681
Si   Siegel, Beatrice
      The sewing machine

DATE DUE			

The Sewing Machine

The *Inventions That Changed Our Lives* series

The Sewing Machine

INVENTIONS THAT CHANGED OUR LIVES

by Beatrice Siegel

WALKER AND COMPANY
New York

For
Rose Sherman and Ann Cooper
—old friends

I would like to thank Barbara S. Janssen, Museum Specialist, Division of Textiles, Smithsonian Institution, Washington, D.C., for patiently answering my questions and for reading the manuscript. I am also indebted to Suzanne E.S. Haines of the Singer Company for her cooperation, and for providing material and photos.

Library of Congress Cataloging in Publication Data

Siegel, Beatrice.
  The sewing machine.

  (Inventions that changed our lives)
  Includes index.
  Summary: Text and illustrations present the invention and development of a machine which liberated people from the drudgery of sewing by hand.
  1. Sewing machines—Juvenile literature. [1. Sewing machines] I. Title. II. Series.
TJ510.S477 1984   681'.7677   83-40397
ISBN 0-8027-6532-7

First published in the United States of America in 1984 by the Walker Publishing Company, Inc.

Published simultaneously in Canada by John Wiley & Sons Canada, Limited, Rexdale, Ontario.

ISBN: 0-8027-6532-7 (reinforced)

Library of Congress Catalog Card Number: 83-40397

This edition printed in 1986.

Printed in the United States of America

10 9 8 7 6 5 4 3 2

CONTENTS

INTRODUCTION

The Eye of the Needle

OUR ANCESTORS still lived in caves when they learned to attach one leaf to another, one animal skin to another. They shaped bone into a tool called an awl with which they punched holes in a piece of animal skin. They then polished and shaped pieces of bone, wood, or ivory into needles. Through the eye of the needle they threaded anything pliable such as sinew or fiber, and laced together two pieces of whatever was at hand. They thus created their first garments. For sewing is an old art, as old as our knowledge of human society.

By the fifth century B.C. craftsmen of the ancient empire of Babylonia fashioned needles out of gold, silver, copper, and bronze. Traders carried the new needles over mountain passes and across plateaus into China. They carried them from port to port down river routes into

Primitive bronze needle.

Greece and Rome, into the ancient lands of Africa, into the Queen's palace in Egypt where, it is said, Cleopatra used a gold needle to embroider a silk garment.

In the era of modern history, the fourteenth century, both the Chinese and Germans—at about the same time—began to use steel for a sharp, durable, inexpensive needle.

All the needles, including those of our earliest ancestors, had a point at one end and an opening—or an eye—at the other.

Not only in ancient times, but in all ages, people handstitched their clothes. Even after land was divided into nation-states and societies became more complex, sewing was done by hand.

By the eighteenth and nineteenth centuries, inventions were bursting upon the world. The cotton gin and water-powered cottonmills were revolutionizing the production of textiles.

Still, everywhere, people continued to stitch everything by hand in the same old way. Sewing was holding back the forward sweep of the textile industry.

By the end of the eighteenth century, clever artisans had already started to put their minds to work on a sewing machine to bring sewing into the modern age. When someone thought up the idea of putting the eye of the needle down near its point, the practical solution for mechanized sewing had taken a giant step forward—though much remained to be done.

1

"Stitch! Stitch! Stitch!"

WHEN ELIAS HOWE, JR. was a grown man he never looked back on his childhood. He did not think it unusual in any way. And indeed it was not, if one thought of farm life in New England, especially in Spencer, Massachusetts, where he was born on July 9, 1819.

More than farming kept the family of parents and eight children busy. Elias's father, after whom he was named, had a grist mill where neighbors brought their grain to be ground. He also had a saw mill that cut tree trunks into lumber.

The income from the farm and the mills was not enough to support the large family. To bring in more money Mr. Howe added another venture to his expanding businesses. He set up a small factory in one of his barns. And that was where Elias, Jr. worked summers and after school from the time he was six years old. He and his sisters and brothers sat for hours each day, hunched over tables, sticking wire teeth into strips of leather. They were making wire brushes, or "cards" as

1

they were called, for the cotton mills springing up all over New England.

Farm life meant hard work and little formal schooling. In his growing up years young Elias knew more about tools and machinery than about reading and writing. He knew how to use a nail and hammer, a saw and axe. He knew that water power turned a big wheel that made the mills work.

Turning out wire brushes made Elias so nimble with his fingers, it sometimes did not bother him that he was lame and could not run as fast as others around the schoolyard and the farm.

He was a thin, curly-headed little boy when his father took him to visit a textile mill in Lowell, Massachusetts. There he saw the way his wire brushes were part of a machine that made cotton into thread. In another room he saw hundreds of women weaving the cotton thread into cloth. They sat at water-powered looms for twelve to fourteen hours a day, producing yards and yards of fabric. It was difficult for the youngster to understand what was done with so much cloth.

At home his mother Polly made most of the items needed by the family. It took her many hours to weave enough cloth on her hand loom for a pair of pants or a dress. And it took her many more hours to stitch the cloth into a garment. His father did the heavier stitching, shaping and sewing together pieces of leather into boots and shoes.

2

The little seamstress.

Everyone in the family, including Elias, knew how to use a needle and thread and stitch a seam. As far as Elias knew, sewing was part of every household. His family and all other farm families sewed their own clothes.

This was so not only on the farm. All over the United States, and all over the world, women, men, and children spent half their waking time sewing by hand in the same way as their ancestors.

For those who earned a living at sewing, it was a life of drudgery. In 1831, there were 74,000 tailors in England. In 1846, in New York City alone, 10,000 women lived by needlework, working twelve to fourteen hours a day for a weekly wage of one dollar and a half. Many tailors and seamstresses became itinerant, traveling to small towns where they were temporarily lodged in wealthy homes while they sewed for the family. They often designed as well as sewed together ornate costumes of handloomed brocade, velvet, silk, and taffeta. Each costume took hundreds of hours of work.

Needleworkers stitched together not only clothes but also tents and uniforms for the army. They sewed leather into boots and saddles. They made church garments, and outfits for fishermen and sailors. They made hats, bags, undergarments, caps, and umbrellas.

People sewed for a living in small chambers of palaces and mansions, or they did piecework at home, or they bent over needle and thread in crowded "manufacturies" (as factories were then called). They suffered crip-

4

Rogman
Sculpsit.
excudebat.

Sewing by hand.

5

pling diseases and damaged eyesight as, night and day, they pushed steel needles through pieces of cloth. They sewed by hand, stitching away the years of their lives. Their misery is described by the English poet, Thomas Hood, in "The Song of the Shirt."

> With fingers weary and worn
> > With eyelids heavy and red,
> A woman sat, in unwomanly rags,
> > Plying her needle and thread,—
> Stitch! stitch! stitch!
> > In poverty, hunger, and dirt;
> And still with a voice of dolorous pitch—
> > Would that its tone could reach the rich!—
> She sang this "Song of the Shirt!"

It hardly made sense that powered looms could produce textiles, while the stitching together of the textiles into consumer products lagged so far behind. There had to be a way to speed up the process of sewing.

While inventors were burrowing their heads in blueprints and models for a sewing machine, Elias Howe, Jr. was feeling the pinch of poverty. At age eleven, his father sent him to "live out" with a neighboring farmer where he worked for his board and keep. His lameness made farm work too taxing and after a year he returned home to work in his father's mills. In 1835, at age sixteen, Elias was ready for the larger world and he left the farm to take a job in a Lowell, Massachusetts factory that made machinery for cotton mills. After a brief stint there and in a hemp carding shop, he moved on to become an apprentice to a Boston master mechanic named Ari Davis. Davis's shop was known as a center for excellent technical repairs and for its collection of nautical instruments.

Among those who came to consult Davis were Harvard college professors who needed mechanical devices for their experiments. Sometimes Elias overheard talk about new inventions that were transforming industry and commerce. A restless search was going on to tap the country's rich resources, to speed up production, and to get rich. Everyone wanted a share of the pie. Elias himself had devised new metal contrivances while he was repairing machines. At age twenty he was feeling confident about his mechanical skills.

In 1839 Elias overheard his employer discuss with two men the reasons why a knitting machine was not working properly.

"What are you bothering yourselves with a knitting machine for?" one man said to the other. "Why don't you make a sewing machine?"

"I wish I could, but it can't be done," the other replied.

"Oh, yes it can," said Ari Davis. "I can make a sewing machine myself," he continued.

"Well," said one of the visitors, a well-known financier, "you do it, Davis, and I'll insure you an independent fortune."

Ari Davis was known as a boastful, eccentric man, and the conversation was dropped.

But Elias Howe remembered that trifling bit of talk four years later. He was twenty-four, married, and the father of three children he supported on a weekly wage of nine dollars a week. It was hardly enough to hold the family together. In addition, each day's work exhausted him, made him feel the weakness of his lame leg. More than once he was too tired to eat dinner and wished only that he could "lie in bed forever and ever."

To bring money into the household his wife Elizabeth had taken in sewing and Elias watched her at night, stitching long hours by dim candlelight, much as his mother had done all her life. His wife was of delicate health, and Elias Howe knew that dramatic measures were needed to change the course of his family's life.

The idea of the "independent fortune" that awaited the inventor of a sewing machine nibbled at his mind. It became a dream, then an obsession. He had no money, but he had determination. To his advantage were qualities nurtured in childhood: discipline and a capacity for hard work.

Evenings he plodded away at a model of a sewing machine. To gain more time, he gave up his job and moved with his family into his parents' home in Cambridge, Massachusetts. He was provided with food and shelter but he had no money for materials to assemble a machine and needed costly items such as metal, wire, and wood.

8

An old friend came to his rescue. George Fisher, a successful merchant, offered to board Elias and his family and supply him with tools, machinery, and five hundred dollars for materials. In return for the investment, Fisher would receive one-half the patent of the machine.

In the attic of Fisher's home, which was converted to a workshop, Howe faced the basic problems of a sewing machine. He had to figure out how a machine could do the following:

Hold the cloth in place.
Feed thread to a needle to provide for regular repeated stitches.
Devise a needle that would take thread through the cloth where it could be tightened underneath in some way, and then have the needle come back up from the cloth.
Provide a repetition of stitches in the proper sequence.

Howe spent hundreds of hours trying to figure out a device to imitate handsewing. He went into shops and observed the way tailors and seamstresses sewed. He carefully observed his wife when she sewed.

A year after he started work, Howe realized that a machine did not have to imitate handsewing, that it might have the possibility of making a new kind of stitch.

Once he had wiped the image of handsewing from his mind and thought of the sewing machine as something entirely different, he was able to proceed with his invention. By then he learned about the accomplishments of others who had been tinkering with devices for mechanized sewing for many years.

2

Early Stages

THE SEARCH for a workable sewing machine was going on, not only in Elias Howe's attic, but in all parts of Europe—in England, Germany, Austria, France, and Scotland. The idea of making something new lured inventors, cabinetmakers, and tailors. Obsessed with their ideas, many deserted their trades, suffered years of poverty, and worked day and night. A few enjoyed the inventive process itself, the idea of creating something new. Most had golden visions of prosperity at the end of the road.

Whatever their purpose, these early inventors did make basic contributions to the sewing machine, but they either neglected to patent their work or their inventions were not practical.

One of the early patents on record to improve sewing belonged to Charles Weisenthal, a German mechanic. In 1775 he received a patent in England for a two-pointed needle with an eye at one end. Thus, Weisenthal could be called the inventor who put the eye of the needle down

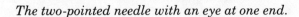

The two-pointed needle with an eye at one end.

near its point. But he did not see the advantage of the eye-pointed needle, that it made it unnecessary for the whole needle to penetrate the cloth in order to make a stitch. His needle, used for embroidery, had to pass completely through the fabric two times. The needle was a failure.

A more solid contribution was made by Thomas Saint, an English cabinetmaker. In 1790 he patented a chainstitch machine that sewed leather. He devised a notched or hooked needle that descended vertically from an overhanging arm into the leather in which holes had been prepunched with an awl. The framework and supporting table were made of wood. The moving parts of the machine were made of metal. He figured out a way of supporting the material in a horizontal position.

Saint provided inventors with a beginning, although he himself never put his ideas to practical use. However, his major contribution to the sewing machine was the perpendicular or vertical needle entering cloth which is supported horizontally.

Little is known about a machine devised by a German, B. Krembs, who in 1810 put together a sewing machine for stitching caps.

12

A few years later, a usable sewing machine that could stitch a seam was patented by Josef Madersperger, a master tailor of Austria. Madersperger's first machine used a two-pointed needle which made a simple running stitch more like embroidery. Later he invented multiple needles for a quilting machine. The threaded needles penetrated the fabric from below, then were drawn back leaving loops on the surface. A thread was drawn through the loops to produce a chain. The machine had serious drawbacks and Madersperger, who had neglected his business, died in a poorhouse.

An important contributor to the sewing machine was a French tailor, Barthelemy Thimmonier, who was completely ignorant about mechanics. Nevertheless, he was convinced that he could invent a mechanical sewing device. After four years during which he put aside his trade and neglected his family, he attained his goal: he invented a workable sewing machine that he and his financial backer patented in 1830.

The machine was useful for embroidery. It used a crochet-style needle with a curved tip, instead of an eye, at the end. The needle descended vertically from an overhanging arm, passed completely through the fabric, and brought up a loop of thread on the barbed end, making a chain stitch on the upper surface of the cloth.

Thimmonier continued to improve his machine to make it practical for regular stitching. He moved from his small hometown of Saint-Etienne to Paris where he

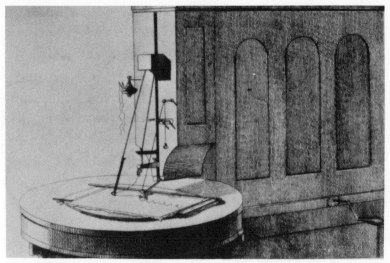

The Madersperger machine.

set up shop. By 1841 he had a factory with eighty machines sewing uniforms for the French army.

The tailors of Paris depended on handsewing for a
livelihood. They saw the sewing machine as competition,
as an invention that would put them out of business. To
avoid the specter of unemployment, they banded together and stormed into Thimmonier's factory late one
night, and smashed every sewing machine. Thimmonier
had to flee for his life.

Undaunted, the young inventor returned to his
hometown where he again set up shop. He continued to
improve his machine, replacing important wood and tin
parts with steel. Backed by a financier, he organized the

14

first sewing machine company with machines that sewed 200 stitches per minute.

Again Thimmonier's factory was attacked and his machines destroyed. That attack and the French Revolution of 1848 put an end to his dream of success in his own country. He traveled to England with one machine rescued from vandals, and was granted a patent there in 1848. In 1850, he took his machine to the United States

Thimonnier and his sewing machine.

where it was also patented. But nothing succeeded, and the great French inventor of the sewing machine, like Madersperger in Austria, died in poverty.

While these inventions were being designed in Europe, a mechanical genius in the United States helped make the sewing machine a U.S. product. A Quaker by the name of Walter Hunt created new items in his shop in New York that made his name a household word. Hunt was not inspired by dreams of wealth or fame. Inventions came easily to him. He had patented such items as the fountain pen, the inkwell, the safety pin, a knife sharpener, a weaving machine, a snow plow, and a heating stove. Long before Elias Howe had struggled in the 1840s to think of the sewing machine as different from handsewing, Walter Hunt had moved in that direction. Between 1832 and 1834, he built three models of sewing machines. In all of them he had the now famous Hunt innovative devices. He put the eye of the needle down near its point. He used two threads, and he used a shuttle.

An eye-pointed curved needle with the upper thread was carried by a vibrating arm. The tip of the needle descended into the cloth and delivered the thread underneath where it formed a loop. A second thread was pulled through the loop by a shuttle. The two threads interlocked and tightened within the seam before the machine went on to form the next stitch. The cloth was supported vertically on a movable frame that had to be

Walter Hunt.

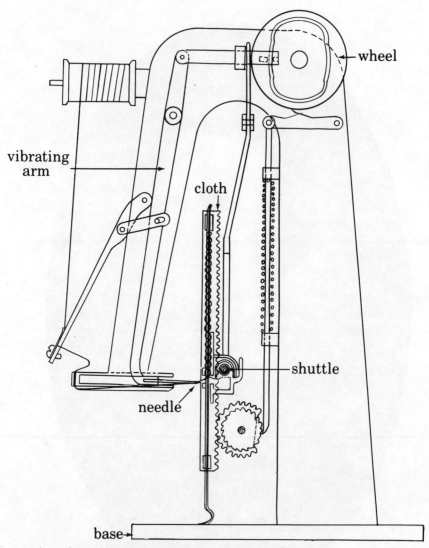

An adapted drawing of Hunt's sewing machine.

18

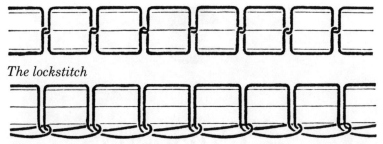

The lockstitch

the single-thread chain stitch.

reset after a short run of stitching. But the eye-pointed needle, the shuttle, and the lockstitch advanced the sewing machine to the level where it could "stitch short, straight seams." It could not sew curved or angular ones.

Hunt's daughter convinced him that his machine would throw seamstresses out of work. Hunt agreed that this was a possibility and did not patent his sewing machine. He simply abandoned it and went on to other inventions.

Therefore, Hunt left in the public domain his great contributions to the progress of the sewing machine: the eye-pointed needle and the lockstitch, which were now accessible to anyone who wanted to use them.

3

A Curiosity

IN 1845 ELIAS HOWE finally produced a model of a sewing machine. It was made of metal. To prove its success, Howe sewed two suits of clothes on it, one for himself and one for his friend George Fisher. The two men became walking models of a successful sewing machine.

A year later Howe patented his machine. He incorporated into it the eye-pointed needle and the lockstitch. It is not clear if Howe did not know of Hunt's invention and created these devices himself, or if he copied them from the Hunt model. Although Elias Howe is generally credited with the invention of the sewing machine, his model resulted from a combination of his own hard work and the contributions of his predecessors, a group of persistent, dedicated people.

Howe's machine, similar in many ways to the Hunt machine, was usable but not entirely practical. The cloth to be sewn hung vertically from pins onto a baster plate. The plate was moved along by a set of gears for a fixed distance after which it had to be reset for another length

20

of cloth. The machine used a curved eye-pointed needle that descended from a vibrating arm. A spool supplied thread to the needle, which carried the thread to the cloth, penetrated the cloth, and left a loop of thread un-

An enlargement of Howe's machine showing cloth pinned to baster plate.

21

derneath. Underneath the plate, a shuttle carrying the second thread passed through the loop, tightening it to form a lockstitch. The machine was powered by a hand wheel.

Here was a mechanical wonder, a sewing machine. Selling it proved to be as difficult as inventing it. Throughout the ordeal of marketing the machine, Elias Howe, Jr. remained a poor, struggling family man, dependent on friends and parents for support.

Howe had no money for advertising, promotion, or education of the public to the labor-saving value of the machine. Nor was he personally an energetic and dynamic man, skilled in the art of salesmanship. And though the times were industrially ripe for such a machine, the public still viewed it as a curiosity, a contraption thrown up by idle hands. No one really thought the machine would be able to replace trained handsewers. Seamstresses and tailors viewed the machine as a threat to their jobs.

In his patient, plodding way, Howe tried to overcome public resistance. He sent out invitations to the best tailors in New England to come and view his machine. One tailor accepted but did not show up.

Howe pushed on. He took his model machine to a Boston garment plant where he sat daily for two weeks at the machine and sewed seams that tailors brought to him. He also participated in a contest between handsewers and the machine. Howe defeated his competitors and proved the machine to be about seven times as fast as handwork. Still, not one machine was sold. The price itself was prohibitive. At three hundred dollars per machine, manufacturers figured they could more profitably employ farm women.

In Washington, where the machine was patented in September, 1846, Howe and Fisher displayed the model in a local exposition. When that only amused the crowd and did not result in a single sale, Howe carried the machine from door to door in the New York garment district.

It seemed hopeless. Fisher, discouraged, withdrew his financial support. Howe moved from Fisher's home back to his parents'.

Howe was as dogged about selling his machine as he had been about inventing it. He convinced his father and older brother Amasa that the solution was in England, an industrial country. His brother undertook the trip abroad. He convinced an English manufacturer of corsets, umbrellas, shoes, and other leather goods that the machine would make greater profits than handworkers would. Mr. William Thomas, quick to see the advantage for his factory where he employed over 5,000 workers, made a deal with Amasa Howe. For 250 pounds, he bought the rights to the machine and won verbal agreement that he would patent the machine in England and pay Howe a royalty for each one sold. In later years, when the sewing machine soared to success, Thomas be-

came a wealthy man on the deal made with Amasa Howe.

In February, 1847, Elias Howe sailed for England (his family joined him at a later date) to work for Thomas for a wage in order to modify his sewing machine for corsets. Arguments between Howe and Thomas ended their relationship.

Desperately poor, Howe and his family moved into a single-room flat. While Howe looked for another backer, his wife, ailing from tuberculosis, became critically ill and returned with the children to Boston. Howe stayed on in London, living from hand to mouth. Finally, he sold the fourth model of a machine he had made in London for a five-pound note, pawned his first machine, paid some bills, and left England to return home. He arrived in Cambridge in time to see his wife before she died.

Back in the states after two years in London, and four years after he patented his invention, Howe was penniless, discouraged, and worn out. But he could perceive the new temper at home. Dramatic changes had taken place in the United States. To his surprise he found that competitors had invented sewing machines that were improvements over his and that machines were being manufactured and sold.

Inventors in the late 1840s and 1850s continued to make important improvements in the sewing machine.

Elias Howe, Jr.

In 1848 John A. Bradshaw created a machine that improved on the workings of the Howe machine. Specifically, he made a better needle and bobbin case which supplied thread to the shuttle. He also introduced a stationary clamp to hold fabric in place instead of the movable baster plate, which he described as "inconvenient and troublesome. . . ."

John Bachelder provided an endless feed belt for the cloth.

Allen B. Wilson devised a shuttle pointed at both ends. It carried a second thread that made a stitch when it went forward and backward. He also figured out a contrivance called a rotating or revolving hook, which would catch and extend the loop of the needle thread and carry it under the bobbin where it locked with the bob-

Wilson's four-motion feed machine.

bin thread. He also added a four-motion cloth feed which moved the cloth forward more effectively than ever before.

Wilson, under the business name of Wheeler and Wilson Manufacturing Company, was the first to make a lightweight machine as a home appliance.

Among those to market a less expensive machine was James A. Gibbs, whose fifty-dollar price tag made his chain stitch machine a popular item.

In 1851 William O. Grover produced a machine that made a two-thread chain stitch.

By far the most aggressive manufacturer of the sewing machine was a man by the name of Isaac Merritt Singer who patented a machine in 1851. Before his patent, Singer began to manufacture and sell sewing machines.

He had just started in business when Elias Howe investigated all the new machines on the market and found that many infringed on his patent rights. Specifically, they all used the eye-pointed needle and the shuttle for the lockstitch. He wrote letters to the manufacturers warning them of their illegal actions and offering to sell them licenses. Backed by a financier who would become joint owner of his patent rights, Howe also prepared a court case against infringers.

Many of the businessmen Howe sued could not afford a legal battle. They came to terms with Howe and agreed to pay him a royalty of twenty-five dollars on each machine they sold. Isaac Singer, however, refused to settle.

While the case against Singer was pending, Howe undertook the manufacture of his machines. At an exhibition at the Castle Garden Fair where he demonstrated a model machine for two weeks, several were sold. In addition, royalty payments gave him temporary control of the industry.

By the time Howe had to face Isaac Singer in court in 1854, he was known as an enterprising and successful businessman.

4

"The Sewing Machine War"

ISAAC MERRITT SINGER was one of the few men capable of mounting a court battle against Elias Howe. He was bold, energetic, imaginative—a man who had made his own way from the age of twelve when he left Pittstown, New York, where he was born in 1811. He took leave of his immigrant German-Jewish parents and seven brothers and sisters and traveled all over the country in search of work. In the following ten years he went from job to job, from town to town, earning a living as a mechanic, cabinetmaker, theater manager, and actor.

At nineteen Singer married and settled in the town of Palmyra, New York, where he and his fifteen-year-old wife Catherine Haley raised a family. To support them Singer again left home to join a small traveling theatrical group.

Isaac M. Singer

The unusual combination of a dramatic flair and mechanical skill propelled the young man to success. He was a flamboyant showman, knowledgeable in all the tricks of winning over an audience. And he was always a tinkerer, playing around with new inventions. During his early years he had patented and put into operation a successful invention for a mechanical excavator for construction. He had also patented a wood carving machine.

When his wanderings were over, Singer settled down in Boston with his family. Like Elias Howe, he took a job in the shop of a master mechanic. And again like Elias Howe, it was at the shop that he was inspired to work on a sewing machine.

When a sewing machine was brought in for repairs, Singer looked it over as a curiosity. He had never seen one before. He analyzed it to find out what was wrong. In the process of repairing it, he redesigned the machine. His work was so innovative that his boss encouraged him to give time to create a new sewing machine. He thought it could be a money-making enterprise.

For eleven days Singer concentrated on the task he set for himself. He worked round the clock, sleeping only two to three hours a night and eating one meal a day. By the end of September, 1850, he had built a model machine for the garment and leather goods industries. He was backed in his enterprise by George Zieber, a publisher and bookseller, and his employer Orson C. Phelps, who gave him the use of his shop. Both men became joint partners with Singer in the manufacture and sale of the first machines before they were even patented.

To demonstrate the heavy machine at church socials and circuses, Singer devised a wooden packing case that became a support for the machine.

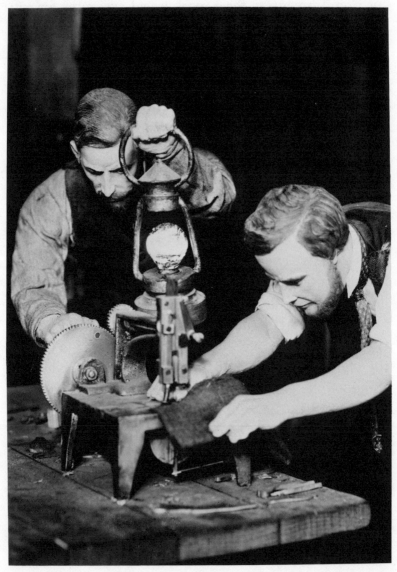

Isaac Singer and his assistant perfecting his machine (diorama).

Here is the way the Singer model machine worked. Singer fashioned a table that held the cloth horizontally instead of having it hang down vertically from a feed bar. He used a wheel feed that pushed the cloth along and provided continuous stitching. He had a shuttle move back and forth in a straight line. In addition, he devised a rotary overhanging shaft that drove a straight needle (instead of a curved one) into the cloth. He also designed a vertical presser foot that held the cloth down when the needle was drawn up. Finally, he worked out a foot treadle to operate the machine, leaving the sewer's hands free to arrange the cloth.

The Singer machine, advertised as an improvement over Howe's, became an instant success. But Singer had also incorporated into his machine the eye-pointed needle and the lockstitch that Howe had already featured on his sewing machine.

Financially backed by industrialist George Bliss, Elias Howe seized on this infringement of his master patent to bring Singer to court. To avoid bitter controversy and expense, other industrialists had settled with Howe. Isaac Singer, however, fought to defend his invention.

For his legal representative he chose a brilliant New York lawyer and financier, Edward Clark. In return for legal services Clark became an equal partner in the firm of I. M. Singer and Company.

Clark claimed that the original inventor of the eye-pointed needle and lockstitch had been Walter Hunt. To prove his case he searched for Hunt and located him. He also located Hunt's model machine in someone's attic. To

The first Singer sewing machine.

strengthen his case Clark persuaded Hunt to rebuild his model machine. After many hours of work, Hunt put together a model made of old parts and new ones. Despite the evidence that Hunt was the original inventor of the eye-pointed needle and the lockstitch, Hunt's neglect to patent his invention swayed the court in favor of Elias Howe.

Thus in 1854 Howe won an unprecedented legal victory. He was declared the original inventor of the sewing machine to whom the public should be "indebted." To compensate for infringement, Singer had to pay Howe fifteen thousand dollars to settle back royalty claims. Further, Howe was to receive a royalty on every sewing machine made and sold in the United States.

Thus Elias Howe, at age 43, was publicly acclaimed the inventor of the sewing machine. His name became famous in the United States and many other parts of the world.

Howe's court victory did not soothe competitive controversy. On the contrary, it inspired others to sue for patent infringements. Howe himself became a defendant in many suits. He was charged with using other inventors' ideas to improve his own machine.

So many court suits pended that the industry was in danger of being destroyed. One newspaper reporter referred to the situation as "the sewing machine war."

To put an end to costly court battles, the head of one firm suggested that the leading sewing machine com-

36

panies pool their patents and interests. In this way they could issue licenses and establish royalty rights without destroying each other. This led to the formation of the "Sewing Machine Combination," a unique business arrangement for its time. It included Howe, Singer, and two other large manufacturers who subsequently controlled the industry. Howe was to receive a royalty of five dollars for every machine sold domestically, and one dollar for every machine exported. He would also share with the others in all the profits of the Combination.

By 1877, when the Combination ceased to exist, the basic features of the sewing machine were available to the public. Open competition led to somewhat lower prices and to the growth of independent manufacturers.

Elias Howe's patents expired in 1867, the year of his death. His profits from the Combination alone, estimated at two million dollars, made him a very rich man.

The first Singer machine in use.

5

A Sewing Machine in Every Home

LIKE A TOUCH of magic, the sewing machine created changes that even its inventors had not envisioned. In itself it revolutionized the home, factory, and industry, and influenced high finance. And folded within the industrial revolution, it contributed to making the United States an industrial giant.

Before these vast changes could take place, the public had to be convinced of the miracles of the sewing machine, to learn that it was a labor-saving device that could eliminate hours of drudgery.

New advertising methods created consumer demand. An avalanche of promotion spilled from posters, billboards, newspapers, and magazines, calling attention to the value of the sewing machine. Customers were lured to carpeted and frescoed showrooms where attractively groomed women demonstrated how easy it was to use the machine. Above all, factory owners finally discovered the machines to be labor saving devices that could increase their profits. Not only were seamstresses and tailors *not* put out of work, but more labor was needed to meet the increased demand for ready-made, low-priced clothing that the sewing machine made possible. One newspaper editor said, "Next to the plow, [the sewing machine] was humanity's most blessed instrument."

As competition increased, manufacturers continued to improve their machines and produce them in attractive designs. The squirrel machine, the horse machine, the cherub, and countless others were consumer bait.

Nothing was holy in the fight for buyers. Machines were identified by names. One was called the "Iron Needle Woman"; another the "Princess of Wales"; and another, the "Common Sense Family Sewing Machine."

Some manufacturers resorted to humor. The Wheeler and Wilson Company printed a cartoon showing a youngster's pants being mended while he was still in them. Others reflected the mores of the time. A favorite ad used a photo of a bride and groom, still in their wedding clothes, admiring a precious gift of a sewing machine aptly named "Domestic."

In promotional skills none was more innovative than Isaac Singer. Indeed he was a pioneer in the art of selling. His company promoted the "Merry Singer,"

The Singer Company showroom.

40

The squirrel machine.

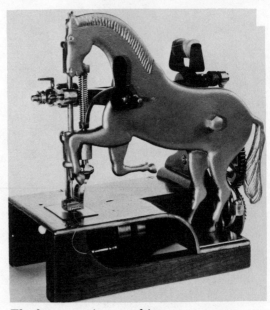

The horse sewing machine.

42

A sewing machine for the bride.

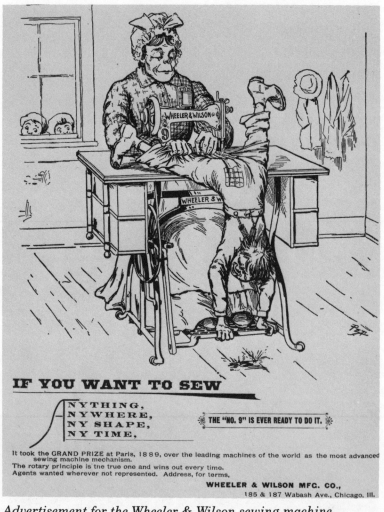

Advertisement for the Wheeler & Wilson sewing machine.

along with a ditty that ran, "I am a Singer—I'm a merry Singer, Singing for you!"

The greatest boost to home sales was the Singer Company's "hire-for-purchase plan." Known as installment buying, it changed consumerism for all time by putting the machine within the range of low-income families. A $100 sewing machine could be purchased for a small down payment of $5 and a guarantee to pay it off at $3 per month.

The Civil War of 1861 helped boost sewing machine sales. The war department required quickly produced uniforms, tents, blankets, boots, and other material. Sewing machine operators in the home and in small factories made it possible to fill orders. Many became wealthy with the construction of new factories and subsidiary industries such as cabinets, needles, machine parts, thread, and other items. By 1863 the sewing machine's 500 stitches a minute made hand sewing with its 30 stitches a minute a thing of the past.

By the end of the Civil War the sewing machine was a fixed product of the industrial age. It made millionaires of some of the inventors who had become manufacturers. Isaac Singer led the list. He had frequently traveled abroad where, after a divorce from his first wife, he married a French woman. He became the center of a social circle noted for lavish living. On the coast of Devon, England, Singer built a mansion called "The Wigwam," at a cost of about half a million dollars. When

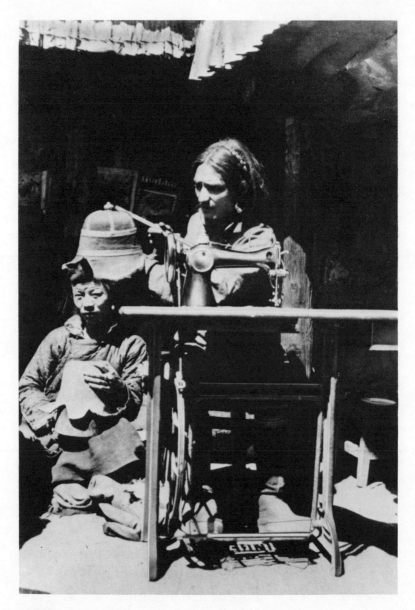

46

he died at age sixty-three, he left an estate estimated at thirteen million dollars.

Isaac Singer and Elias Howe bequeathed more than their private fortunes. The sewing machines they invented and promoted revolutionized the social structure as well as the economy.

A Seminole Indian sewing a dress.

A hat-maker using a sewing machine in Tibet.

47

U.S.-made sewing machines were exported to Africa, Tibet, India, France, Italy, and Japan. They changed the lives of people in the most remote corners of the world. As the first home appliance, half the human race was relieved of the stress of handsewing. People moved into other forms of employment. The owner of a machine could become an entrepreneur, sewing for the community.

The greatest boost was to factory manufacture of ready-to-wear clothing. Factories were established in urban centers and along transportation routes, turning out clothing priced within the range of all classes of people. The clothes were well made, practical, and comfortable.

The sewing machine made life easier for millions. On the other hand, the factory system brought with it its own forms of evil. Women, in particular, freed from being needleworkers within their homes, entered the garment industry in increasing numbers. The needle trades also attracted immigrant labor. Many set up home factories in their broken down flats where families, including children, worked at sweated labor. Others put in ten-hour days, six days a week, in crowded, dirty, fire-trap factory buildings.

Thomas Hood, in his poem "Song of the Shirt," had described conditions of hand-needleworkers. In the factory period, the fate of workers was described by an immigrant Polish poet, Morris Rosenfeld, in his poem, "The Sweatshop."

So wild is the roar of the machines in the
  sweatshops,
I often forget I'm alive—in the din.
I'm drowned in the tide of the terrible tumult
My ego is slain; I become a machine.
I work, and I work, without rhyme, without
  reason
Produce, and produce, and produce without
  end.
For what? and for whom? I don't know, I don't
  wonder—

*Clothing industry sweatshop photo of original painting by
William Gropper.*

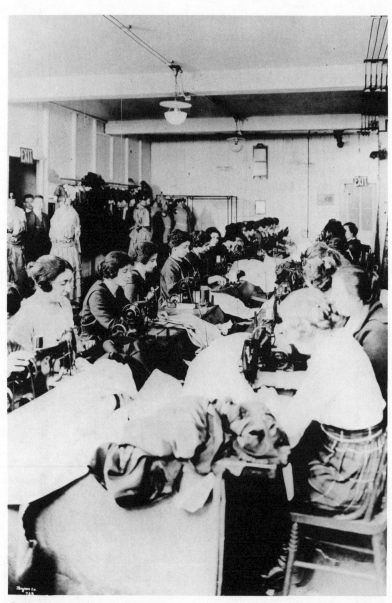

Garment workers at machines.

Since when can a whirling machine
   comprehend?

Factory conditions in the garment industry gave rise to a liberal and radical working class who fought for their rights and for the benefits of industrial society. Labor history was made with the first women's strike in the shirtwaist industry in 1909 when 20,000 women walked out of factories demanding better working conditions.

Middle-class women, on the other hand, relieved of the household chores, especially the sewing and designing of clothes, became ladies of leisure. They developed other interests, entered the political, social, and economic arenas. In the larger world they shed nurtured attitudes of submissiveness and began to speak out. They demanded the right to vote, to take part in social reform, to enter colleges and to become doctors and lawyers. The sewing machine is credited in part with this changed perspective, for not until women were freed from household drudgery did they realize how narrow and hampered their lives had been.

The sewing machine, slow to get started, kept pace with new technology. From year to year the machine was changed, refined, given more tasks. Sewing machines could do embroidery, bindings, buttonholes. By 1882, machines could produce sixty-eight varieties of stitches. In 1890, machines could be powered by electricity.

51

The industry continued to grow so that by the end of the nineteenth century there were 125 companies producing sewing machines with a yearly production valued at over twenty-one million dollars. Not all these companies stayed in business. Singer absorbed many competitors and continued to dominate the industry. In 1906, as if to symbolize its supremacy, the Singer Company built a forty-seven-story building for its executive offices, giving New York its first skyscraper and the tallest building in the world.

The sewing machine remained a U.S. product until foreign competition, notably from Japan and Western Europe, cut into the U.S. market. By the 1960s no more than sixty sewing machine companies existed in the United States.

Research to speed up the machine's capacity and reduce the physical labor of its operators continues today. The advanced sewing machine is now hooked into the electronic age. The latest machine has a built-in electronic system and a micro-computer. A stitch is selected from a choice of over twenty stitches that are preprogrammed into the machine, then a button is touched, and one machine will sew programmed lengths and widths on sheer or heavy fabrics; sew cuffs or sleeves; make buttonholes; do decorative stitches; or run up a straight seam.

Thus the industry has served notice that, by adapting to the computer age, the sewing machine is here to stay.

52

The electronic sewing machine.

*The Singer Building
completed in 1908.*

Photo credits

The author gratefully acknowledges permission from the following sources to reprint photographs on the following pages: Library of Congress collections (p. 43); Picture Collection, the Branch Libraries, New York Public Library (pp. 3, 5); Science Museum, London (p. 19); The Singer Company (pp. 30, 36, 40, 41, 46, 47, 53); Sophie Gropper (p. 49); the Photo Library Department, Museum of the City of New York (photograph by Byron on p. 50); The Smithsonian Institution (photo numbers 1379-A p. vi, 83-4688 p. 12, 49373 p. 14, 10569-C p. 15, 32066 p. 17, 42554 p. 18, 33493 p. 21, 622 p. 24, 45504 p. 26, 34182 p. 32, 45572-D p. 34, 45505-C p. 42, 53112 p. 42, 73-8012 p. 44).

Author's Notes

I would like to credit the following books for important resource material:

Roger Burlingame. *March of the Iron Men: A Social History of Union Through Invention.* New York: Charles Scribner's Sons, 1938.

Grace Rogers Cooper. *The Sewing Machine: Its Invention and Development.* Washington, D.C.: Smithsonian Institution Press, 1976.

William Ewers and H. W. Baylor. *Sincere's History of the Sewing Machine.* Phoenix, Arizona: Sincere Press, 1970.

The Thomas Hood poem, "Song of the Shirt," appears in *The Servant in the House: A Brief History of the Sewing Machine* by Frederick L. Lewton, reprinted by permission of the Smithsonian Institution, Washington, D.C. by the Singer Manufacturing Company.

The Morris Rosenfeld poem, "The Sweatshop," appears in *Songs of Labor and Other Poems*, translated from the Yiddish by Rose Pastor Stokes and Helena Frank, Boston: Richard G. Badger, 1914.

Index

Africa, *vii*, 48
Austria, 13

Babylonia, *vi*
Bachelder, John, 26
Bliss, George, 33
Boston, Massachusetts, 7
Bradshaw, John A., 26

Cambridge, Massachusetts, 8, 25
Cards, 1
China, *vi–vii*
Civil War, 45
Clark, Edward, 33-35
Cleopatra, *vii*

Davis, Ari, 7–8
"Domestic" sewing machine, 39, 43

Egypt, *vii*
England, 4, 11, 12, 15, 23–25, 45

Fisher, George, 9, 20, 23
France, 13–15, 48
French Revolution of 1848, 15

Germany, *vii*, 11, 12
Gibbs, James A., 27
Greece, *vii*
Grover, William O., 27

Harvard, 7
Hood, Thomas, 6, 48
Howe, Amasa, 23
Howe, Elias, Jr., 1-11, 16, 20–25, 27–29, 33–37, 47
    childhood, 1–6
    develops sewing machine, 8–11, 20, 22
    royalties, 28, 35, 37
Howe, Elizabeth, 8
Hunt, Walter, 16-19, 20, 34-35

I.M. Singer & Co., 33, 39–41, 45, 53
India, 48
Italy, 48

Japan, 48, 52

Knitting machine, 7
Krembs, B., 12

Lowell, Massachusetts, 6

Madersperger, Josef, 13, 14
"Merry Singer" sewing machine, 39

Needles, *vi-vii*, 9, 11–12, 13, 16–19, 20–22, 27, 33, 34–35
New York City, 4, 23, 52

Palmyra, New York, 29
Patents, 9, 11, 13, 15, 19, 23, 27–29, 31, 33–35
Phelps, Orson C., 31
Pittstown, New York, 29

Rome, *vii*
Rosenfeld, Morris, 48–49

Saint, Thomas, 12
Sewing by hand, *vi-vii*, 2–6, 8–9, 45
    for a living, 4–6, 8, 14, 22
Sewing machine:
    advertising of, 22, 33, 38-45
    baster plate, 20, 21, 26
    binding, 51
    bobbin, 26–27
    buttonholes, 51, 52
    chainstitch, 12, 13, 19, 27
    cloth feed, 26, 27, 33
    cost, 23, 27, 37, 45
    destruction of, 14–15
    electric, 51